LET'S IMAGINE:
ELECTRICITY

Tom Johnston
Illustrated by Sarah Pooley

'To imagine is everything.' Einstein

THE BODLEY HEAD
London

IN THE SAME SERIES
Air
Colour
Energy
Forces
Water

British Library Cataloguing
in Publication Data
Johnston, Tom
Electricity.—(Let's imagine)
1. Electricity—Juvenile literature
I. Title   II. Pooley, Sarah   III. Series
537   QC527.2
ISBN 0-370-30866-2

Text © Tom Johnston 1986
Illustrations © Sarah Pooley 1986
Printed and bound in Great Britain for
The Bodley Head Ltd
30 Bedford Square, London WC1B 3RP
by William Clowes Ltd, Beccles
First Published 1986

The discovery of electricity is probably the thing that has most affected our lives over the last few hundred years. People have been investigating electricity for hundreds of years. About 600 B.C. a Greek called Thales found that if he rubbed a piece of amber, he could make small objects stick to it. Amber is a sort of natural plastic, and you can do a similar experiment by rubbing a plastic pen and picking up small pieces of paper with it. About 1570 A.D., William Gilbert, doctor to Queen Elizabeth I of England, carried out similar experiments. He named the effects that he saw electricity, after the Greek word for amber, elektron.

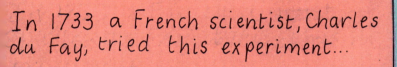

In 1733 a French scientist, Charles du Fay, tried this experiment...

If two amber beads are suspended on string and then rubbed...

...they repel each other and are driven apart!

The same happens with two glass beads.

But if one amber bead and one glass bead are rubbed and held close — they attract one another!

Mr du Fay had discovered that there are two kinds of electric charge — positive and negative.

You can even use this same rubbing effect to produce electric sparks. Wearing a nylon shirt and a woollen jumper, stand in a dark room in front of a mirror. Pull the jumper off and sparks will fly between the shirt and jumper.

These sparks are caused by electric charges leaping through the air. This is exactly what happens when you see lightning during thunderstorms. Inside clouds there are tiny particles of water, ice and air. The friction caused between these particles when they rub together builds up to form an electric charge. When a great number of charges collect, they can leap through the air as a large lightning spark. The sparks leap from cloud to cloud, or from a cloud to the ground.

In 1801 Alessandro Volta presented one of the first electric batteries to Napoleon.

Well done, Volta!

The electrical measurement 'volt' is named after Volta, because of his experiments with electricity.

About 45 years later, an Italian scientist, Alessandro Volta, invented an easier way of producing electricity – the battery. He did this by putting a piece of paper, soaked in salt water, between two small pieces of metal – one copper and the other zinc. He attached a wire to each of these and placed the ends of the wires against his tongue. This made his tongue tingle.

Volta then piled lots of the batteries on top of each other, so that the copper piece of the one below touched the zinc piece of the one above. This gave off enough electricity to produce a spark when the ends of the wires were brought together.

You can make a battery very like Volta's. Soak a piece of paper in water and sandwich this between a piece of tin foil and a copper coin.

Attach a wire to each piece of metal and test the ends against your tongue. Oooh! It tingles!

paper soaked in salt water — tin foil — copper coin

Modern batteries are really just like Volta's. If you have an old, used 1.5 volt battery, cut it open to see what is inside. Once you have cut through the protective metal case, it will come apart fairly easily.

You will see it has a zinc case inside, just like Volta's piece of zinc, but instead of the piece of copper, it has a rod of carbon. Between the carbon and zinc, Volta's salt water has been replaced with an acid paste.

This is a 1.5 volt battery or cell. A larger battery, such as a 9v one, is really just six 1.5v cells joined together.

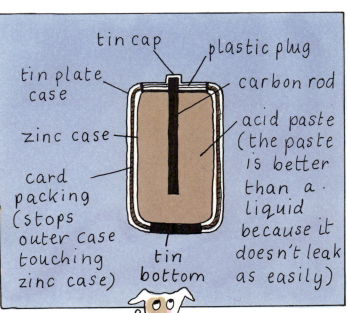

tin cap
plastic plug
tin plate case
carbon rod
zinc case
acid paste (the paste is better than a liquid because it doesn't leak as easily)
card packing (stops outer case touching zinc case)
tin bottom

How many 1.5 cells in a 12V battery?

ANSWER: 8

If you leave batteries in a radio or torch unused for a long time, they will leak and the acid will corrode the metal parts of the torch.

Have you ever heard of getting electricity from a piece of fruit?

You can use the zinc and carbon from the battery to make some unusual batteries of your own. Using scissors, cut the zinc into 1 cm wide strips. You'll need several carbon rods, but you don't need to cut open more batteries for these. The 'lead' inside pencils is really carbon, so you can use this instead. Now you need two pieces of wire (any thin wire will do), a small 1.5 volt bulb in a holder and a lemon. Stick a piece of zinc and a carbon rod into the lemon, keeping them about 2 cm apart. Attach a wire to the top of each (paper clips are very useful for attaching wires) and then fix the other ends of the wires to your bulb holder, as shown in the diagram. The bulb should light up. The juice in the lemon acts just like Volta's salt water, or the acid in a battery.

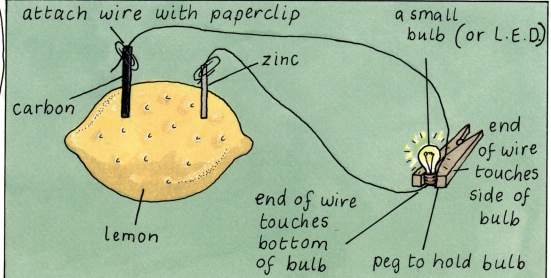

You can buy L.E.D.s in the lighting department of a big store or a toyshop.

Try the tingle test on your tongue as well!

✱ You could use a L.E.D. (Light Emitting Diode) instead of a light bulb. It needs less electric current to make it light up.

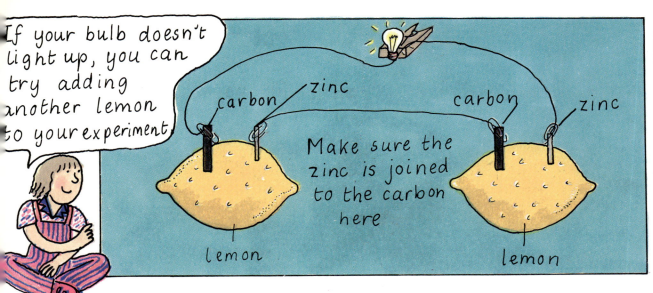

You can also do this experiment, using potatoes, onions, apples or oranges, instead of lemons. You would need three potatoes to light one L.E.D. and about ten potatoes to light one light bulb.

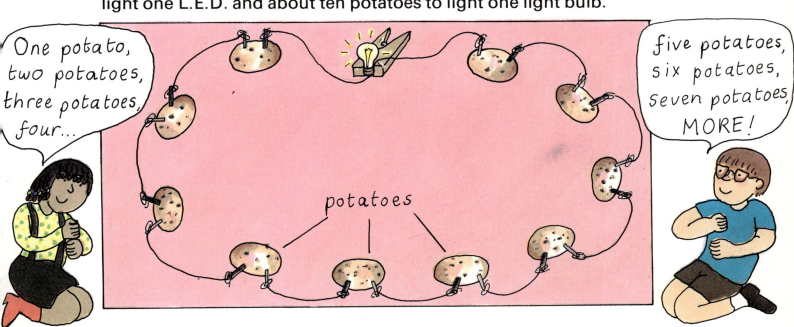

Fruit and vegetables are not the only things we can get electricity from. Some animals produce their own electricity. The electric catfish, the electric ray and the electric eel, for example, can produce shocks that can stun or kill their prey. The South American electric eel can stun a horse as it crosses a river, and shocks from eels have been measured as high as 550 volts.

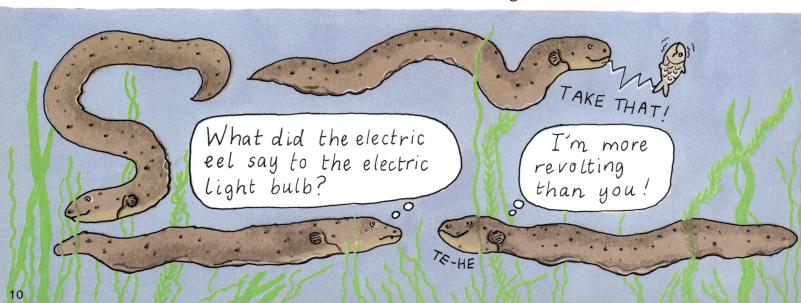

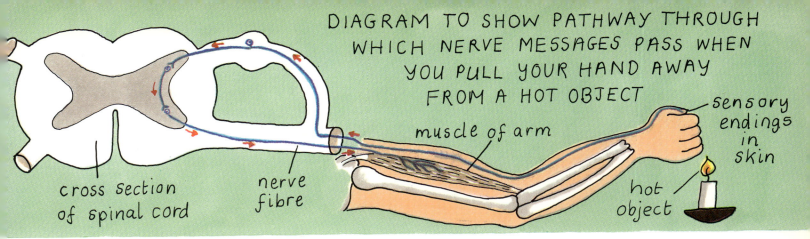

Even your body can produce electricity. In fact it uses electricity to pass signals around it, in much the same way as a computer does. Your nerves, which are long, thin fibres, can produce small electric charges, which travel along one nerve and on to the next one – rather like electricity passing through wiring in a circuit. These electric charges travel very fast. If you step on a pin, the message from your foot takes only .05 of a second to reach your spinal cord, return to your foot and make your muscle move the foot. Your brain also produces very, very tiny electric currents, but these are so tiny that it would take about 30 million of them to light up a small torch bulb!

To make any battery work you need to have a circuit, that is an unbroken piece of wire that links one end (terminal) of your battery to the other end.

You can show this with a 1.5 volt bulb, three wires and a 1.5 volt battery. Connect them to make a circuit and they will work, but leave a gap anywhere and the bulb will not light up.

This gap in the circuit can be quite useful as a switch for turning the circuit on or off.

When the switch is off, the contacts are open. There is a gap in the electrical circuit.

When the switch is turned on, the spring bends, forcing the contacts to close. This makes a complete electrical circuit.

"The French King, Louis XV, when experimenting with electricity accidentally gave a shock to 700 monks who were joined hand to hand!"

Electricity only flows round complete circuits and through certain substances. You can use a circuit with a gap to test which substances will let electricity pass through them. Set up your experiment like this:

"If the bulb lights up, then electricity is getting through!"

Object e.g. iron nail, wired to gap.

"Try as many different things as you can find... try paper, plastic, tin foil, pencil lead, etc!"

It is only recently that scientists have had a better understanding of exactly what electricity is. Everything is made up of tiny bits called atoms. Atoms themselves are made up of even smaller bits, and one of these smaller bits is called the electron. Electrons can break away from atoms. Substances that let electricity flow through them have free electrons which can move – this is the electricity flowing. It is a build-up of electrons on the surface of things that causes the sparks we mentioned earlier.

The most simple atom is the hydrogen atom. It has one electron in orbit round its nucleus.

electron   nucleus

A carbon atom has six electrons circling the nucleus.

If something lets electricity pass through it, we call it a conductor. From the experiment on page 13 you probably found that most metals are conductors. Things like paper and plastic won't conduct very well, so we call them insulators. This is why electric wires are usually covered in plastic. The plastic insulates the wire, so that electricity cannot flow out of it into the things it touches.

We can use conductors and insulators to make an electrical game. This is a quiz-board and needs a 1.5 volt battery and bulb. You also need two wires and some strips of tin foil for conductors. You can use sticky tape as an insulator.

The front of the board has questions down one side and answers jumbled down the other. The back of the board has to be set up so that the bulb will light up when the correct question and answer are joined together.

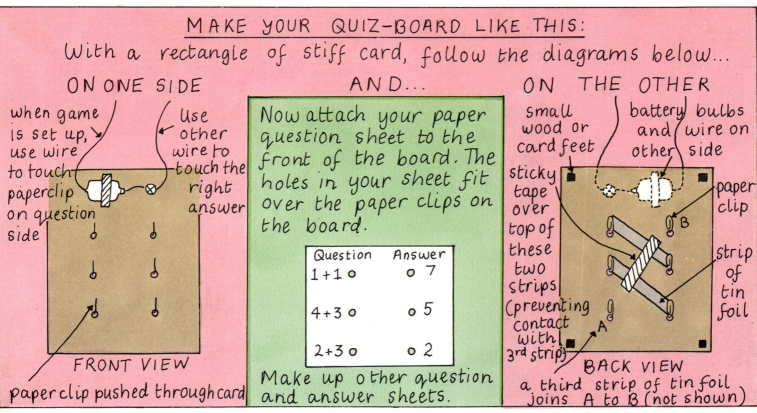

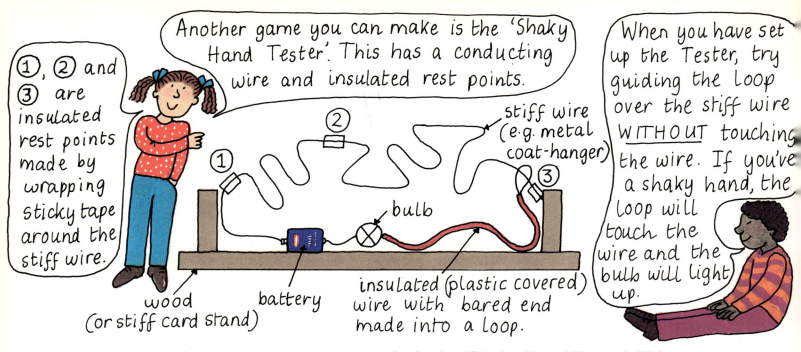

Another game you can make is the 'Shaky Hand Tester'. This has a conducting wire and insulated rest points.

Not all conductors are equally good at letting electricity pass through them. Wires that let the current (flow of electricity) pass through easily are called low resistors. Those that it's harder for the current to flow through are called high resistors. Try this experiment with some high-resisting wire. If you pluck some strands from a metal pan-scouring soap pad, this will give you the wire you need. Wash the soap off before you use it.

Set up experiment as follows...

ⓐ Take a block of wood and attach the fine wires from the pan-scourer to it, using drawing-pins to fix the wires firmly.

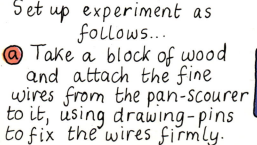
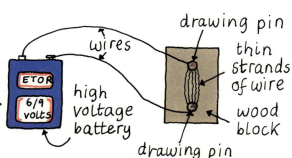

ⓑ Attach a conducting wire to each drawing-pin
ⓒ Now attach the other ends of your conducting wires to the battery. Watch what happens!

"The resistance of a wire depends on what it's made of, how long it is and how thin."

"The wire in our experiment was very thin and made of iron —so it burnt very easily."

Your wire will have burned. All wires get slightly warm when electricity passes through them. The higher their resistance, the warmer they get. The very thin wire strands you used in the experiment got so hot that they melted. This could be very dangerous, and to stop wires overheating like this, the mains circuits in houses have fuses in them. If the wiring gets too hot, the fuse melts. A fuse is made from a piece of wire that melts easily like tin. The piece of tin is kept inside a glass cylinder so that if it does melt, it can't start a fire. Have a look inside a plug that isn't being used and you will see a fuse.

"Earth is for safety."

"The live and neutral wires carry the electricity."

"This is a cord grip. It holds the flex in place."

"Have you ever felt like blowing a fuse...!?"

"This is the fuse. Underneath the casing is a thin strand of fuse wire."

① Green/yellow EARTH
② Blue NEUTRAL
Brown LIVE

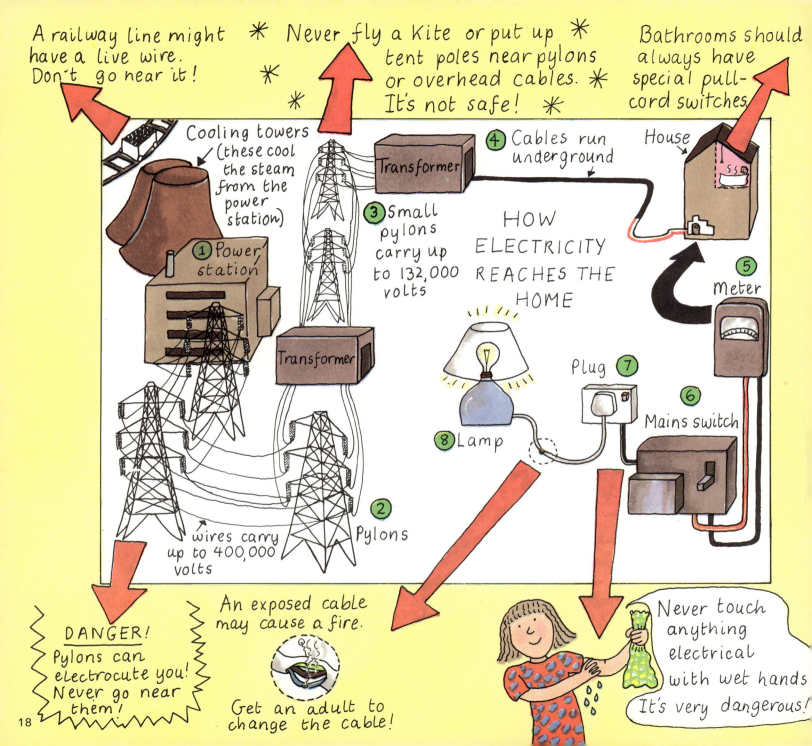

Whenever you switch on an electric fire or cooker you are using this same heating effect. In both of these appliances part of the circuit is a conductor with a high resistance. In an electric fire, you can see this as a thin wire wound around a porcelain bar. This gets so hot that it has to be protected by a guard to stop things touching it.

The reason ordinary circuit wire doesn't melt is because it is made of copper which is a good conductor and does not get too hot. The heating element of a fire is made from nichrome wire, which can get red hot without melting.

Over 100 years ago, the first street lamps were lit up. They were electric arc lamps and used the same principle as the electric heater and cooker.

THE FIRST LIGHT BULBS

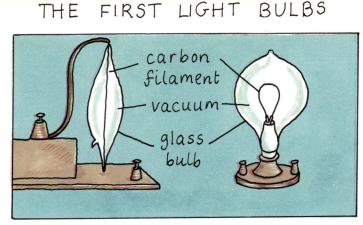

The electric arc lamps did have some disadvantages. They became very hot and gave off smoke. A more satisfactory solution was found by Edison and Swan. Their inventions were very similar to the bulb we use today.

Another appliance that uses the heating effect is the light bulb. This was first invented simultaneously in 1878 by Thomas Edison in the US and Joseph Swan in Britain. The wire filament that you can see inside a light bulb has a high resistance. It gets so hot that it glows white, giving out light. This filament is made of a metal called tungsten. Although the tungsten will not melt at this great heat, it would react with the oxygen in the air and burn. So, to stop this happening the bulb is filled with a non-reacting gas called argon.

Electricity is very closely linked to magnetism. To show this you need a small bar magnet and a compass. If you put the compass near the magnet, it will point in a different direction, instead of pointing north.

You can now do the same thing to the compass needle without using a magnet. Use a 6 volt battery for this, or four 1.5 volt ones, each joined top to bottom. Join a long piece of wire from one battery terminal to the other. Wrap part of the wire tightly around a pencil to make a coil. Pull the pencil out. Now if you put a compass near the coil, the needle will change direction just as it did when it was placed near the magnet.

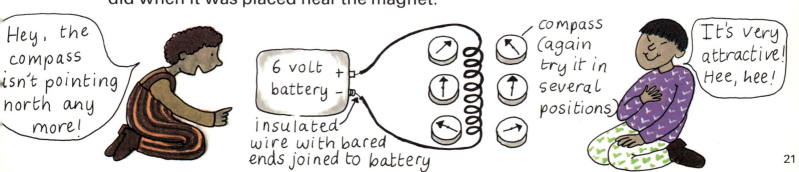

Both the magnet and coil affect the compass because they have a magnetic field around them. This is invisible, but we can see it if we use some iron filings.

Place the magnet under a thin piece of paper and sprinkle the filings on top of the paper. Give a few gentle taps to the paper and you will see an interesting pattern start to form. The coil makes the same pattern.

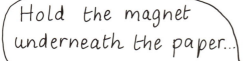

Hold the magnet underneath the paper...

Look what happens... the filings form this pattern.

When you've finished showing the magnetic field, you can have some fun... How? By making funny faces!

Draw a face on a piece of paper. Put some iron filings on the paper and using the magnet (under the paper), move the filings to make a beard, hair or eyebrows.

The coil you have made could be called an electromagnet. It's not very strong, but if you put an iron nail through the centre of the coil it gets stronger. Try using it to lift up some small iron tacks.

Some animals can also produce magnetic fields. A strange-looking fish, called the Mormyrid, from Central Africa, can do this. It has eyes that can barely see and a trunk-like snout. In its long, pointed tail it has a group of muscles, which can produce electricity in short pulses, making its tail negative and its head positive. This produces a magnetic field around the fish, which the fish uses to "sense" objects around it as it moves.

The first electromagnet was made by William Sturgeon in 1825. You can use your electromagnet to make an electric bell. Here is one way of doing it:

When you tap the switch, the circuit is complete and the nail is magnetised. This attracts the iron piece and bends the ruler, banging the metal lump against the can or bell top. It rings! Take your finger off the switch — the nail releases and the ruler swings back!

Samuel Morse used an electromagnet when he invented the telegraph in 1835. This had a buzzer that worked rather like your bell. Of course to send messages over large distances the wires between the buzzer and tap switch had to be hundreds of kilometres long.

--/..../.-/-
-/-- ..
../.-/-.-/
./-./---.?

THE MORSE CODE												
A	B	C	D	E	F	G	H	I	J	K	L	M
.-	-...	-.-.	-..	.	..-.	--.	....	..	.---	-.-	.-..	--
N	O	P	Q	R	S	T	U	V	W	X	Y	Z
-.	---	.--.	--.-	.-.	...	-	..-	...-	.--	-..-	-.--	--..

"When you speak to someone on the phone, an electric signal goes from the mouthpiece. It travels along wires to the other telephone...

...where it works the earpiece, so that the other person hears you then talks back to you in the same way."

earpiece (receiver)
electromagnets
sound waves
mouthpiece (microphone)

Although it's more complicated than the telegraph, the telephone works in a similar way using electromagnets. This was developed by Alexander Graham Bell in 1876. About the same time, another dedicated scientist, Michael Faraday, found a way of using magnetism to make electricity, when he invented the dynamo in 1831.

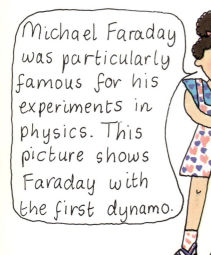

"Michael Faraday was particularly famous for his experiments in physics. This picture shows Faraday with the first dynamo."

disc
coil

"Faraday was also professor of chemistry at the Royal Institution, London, for thirty years. Scientists sometimes called him 'the Father of Electricity'."

Some bicycles have dynamos instead of batteries to provide power for the lights. Unlike batteries, a dynamo doesn't run out, but if you stop moving, the lights go out. Inside a dynamo there is a magnet, bent so both poles face inwards. Between the poles is a coil of wire. If the wire coil is moved, by the bicycle wheel turning, then electricity starts to flow through the wire.

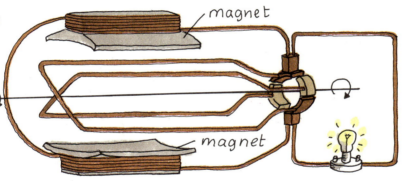

In a simple electric dynamo, a coil of wire is turned clockwise by mechanical energy (you moving the pedals).

The coil lies between opposite poles (N and S) of two magnets. This causes a flow of electric current in the coil as it rotates and lights the bulb.

Inside power stations, there are large dynamos called generators. These make vast amounts of electricity. They are driven by steam engines fuelled by oil, coal or nuclear power.

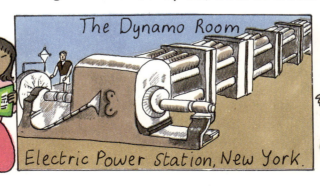

It was many years after Faraday's discovery before the results of his work were used. But in 1882 things were to change.

Thomas A. Edison built the first large power station in New York. Others were built in England. At last there was power for the people!

If you have a toy electric train or car at home, open it up and look inside. You will see what looks like a dynamo. In fact it's an electric motor. We could say that a motor is just a dynamo used in a different way. In a dynamo you turn a wire coil inside a magnetic field to make electricity. In a motor you pass electricity through the wire coil and it spins. Motors like this can be powerful enough to turn the wheels on a vehicle the size of a milkfloat.

The dynamo made large amounts of electricity available for the first time. Inventors soon began to put this to use. The telegraph and telephone inventions were followed by Edison's phonograph (an early record player) in 1877 and William Crookes' cathode ray tube (later used in TV) in 1878.

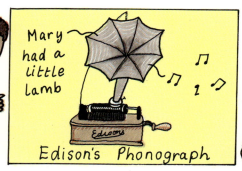

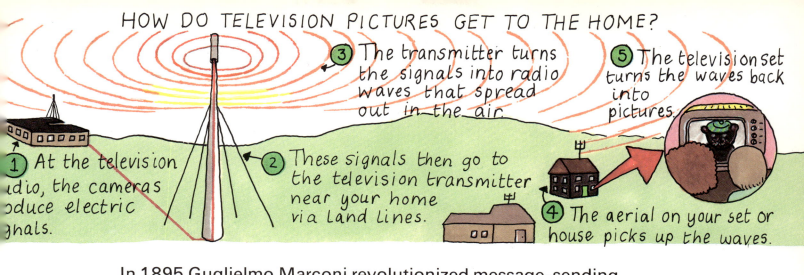

In 1895 Guglielmo Marconi revolutionized message-sending with the invention of the radio. Of course many other scientists were involved in this work. Their inventions and discoveries eventually allowed John Logie Baird (in Britain) and Vladimir Zworykin (in the US) to develop a way of sending pictures by radio waves. This was television.

It would be difficult for you to make a TV or radio transmitter in your home, but you can use electricity to send messages like this:

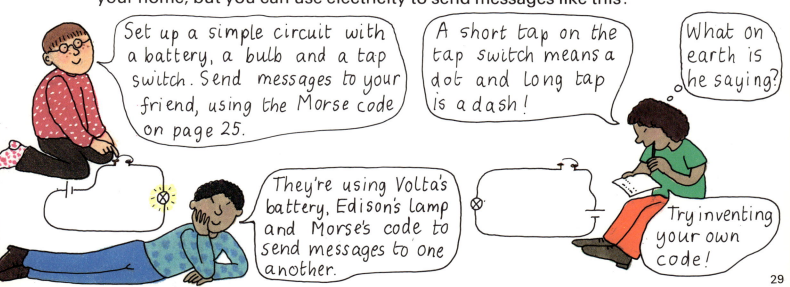

Since the 1940s, and especially in the last ten years, there has been a further revolution in the use of electricity with the development of electronics and microelectronics. These work basically in the same way as the electric circuits you have been using, but they are extremely small, so small, in fact, that many hundreds of circuits could be fitted into an area the size of a postage stamp. These circuits are printed on silicon and so are called "silicon chips" or "microchips".

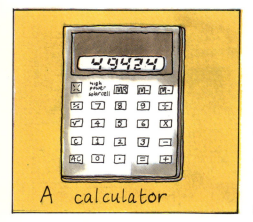

Electronics has allowed the development of many new tools and machines. One of the most important of these is the new generation of computers that use very small circuits called "integrated circuits". These can store, use and process information at incredible speed. Computer use is becoming widespread and micro-computers are finding their way into many people's homes. With all these exciting developments taking place, we can barely imagine what uses electricity will be put to in the future!

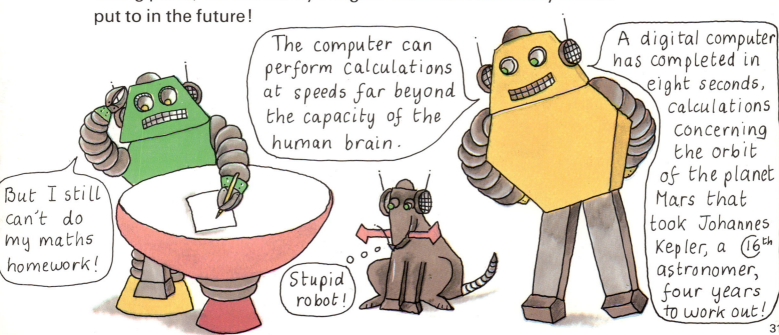

INDEX

Aiken, Howard, 31
Atoms, 13

Babbage, Charles, 31
Baird, John Logie, 29
Batteries, 6–9, 12, 25
Bell, Alexander Graham, 26

Cathode ray tube, 28
Circuits, 11, 12–13, 17, 19, 23, 25, 30, 31
Computers, 31
Conductors, 5, 14–16, 19
Crookes, William, 28

Dynamo, 26–28

Edison, Thomas, 20, 27, 28, 29
Electric bell, 25
Electric charge, 3, 4, 5, 11, 14
Electric shock, 10, 13
Electromagnet, 23–26

Electronics, 30–1
Electrons, 13

Faraday, Michael, 26, 27
Fay, Charles du, 3
Franklin, Benjamin, 5, 14
Fuses, 17

Gilbert, William, 3

Heating effect, 17, 19–20

Insulators, 14–16, 19

Light bulb, 20
Lightning, 4–5, 14

Magnetism, 21–28
Marconi, Guglielmo, 29
Microchips, 30
Morse, Samuel, 25, 29
Morse code, 25, 29

Phonograph, 28
Plugs, 17, 18

Quiz-board, 15

Radio, 29
Resistors, 16–17, 19, 20

Sturgeon, William, 25
Swan, Joseph, 20

Telegraph, 25
Telephone, 26
Television, 29
Thales, 3

Volt, 6
Volta, Alessandro, 6, 7, 8, 29

Zworykin, Vladimir, 29